8 Reasons Why Forex Trading Hasn't Replaced Your Full Time Job Yet
(and How to Fix It Fast)

Written by: MJ Worthmore

WORTHMORE FAMILY MEDIA
PUBLISHING

COPYRIGHT © 2023 MARQUES-JEREMIAH B. WORTHMORE SR.
All rights reserved.

8 Reasons Why Forex Trading Hasn't Replaced Your Full Time Job Yet
(and How to Fix It Fast)

ISBN 979-8-3940-4052-8   *Paperback*

Dedication

To Gloria, my mother. You're the reason I became who I am.

Table of Contents

Introduction: Why This Will Improve Your Trading When You Implement It

Reason Number 1: Little to No Understanding of Fundamental Drivers

Reason Number 2: Little to No Clear Understanding of Smart Money Concepts

Reason Number 3: You Have No Trade Entry Formula

Reason Number 4: You Have No Trade Management Plan

Reason Number 5: You Have No Clear Understanding of Risk to Reward Ratios

Reason Number 6: Little to No Understanding of How to Control Risk

Reason Number 7: You Have No "Pull Me Away from the Table" Number

Reason Number 8: You Have No Coaching and Accountability

Why This Will Improve Your Trading When You Implement It

The reason this is going to immediately improve your trading is because in this book, I'm going to tell you EXACTLY what's keeping you from earning the kind of income you want as a Forex Trader…

And then give you the opportunity to learn how to do the opposite of what hasn't been working for you.

As you can already tell, this is a small book; one that you can read from cover to cover in just one sitting. This book is not an autobiography, but a guide designed to help you take actionable steps, right away. Because of that, you'll find no fluff or fillers within these pages…

Just pure, concise and relevant information that you can apply immediately and begin to see results within a matter of days, if not hours.

In a world full of overly recycled and unclear information, once you're able to fully understand all of the places you've gone wrong with your current strategy or trading system…

Then and only then will you be able to instantly correct your course, stop doing the wrong things and start doing the right things.

And THAT will be when your trading results make a complete 180° turn in the right direction.

The truth is, trading forex without having a true understanding of how the market "actually works" isn't trading at all: **It's Gambling.**

Your ability to get into and out of a trade with "The Big Money Movers" is the lifeblood of your trading and your golden ticket to bigger paydays.

After you read this, and begin to take the necessary actions to correct these common mistakes, you'll find that you won't have to worry about whether or not you'll be able to catch pips and secure profits anymore.

But this is true, only if you're willing to implement the steps and do what's required, moving forward.

So, Who am I and Why listen to me?

My name is Marques-Jeremiah Worthmore.

You can call me Coach MJ.

I am an Author and Full Time Forex Trader, that's funded with multiple Prop Firms and private investors; earning 5 Figures (in profit) on a monthly basis.

I am also the CEO and Founder of **Legal Con Artist University**; *an online educational platform that specializes in helping traders get and maintain multiple 6-Figure Funded Accounts through various Prop Firms and live off their trading profits.*

I've been living off of my trading profits for the last two and a half years and I've personally helped close to two dozen people within the last 12 months become six figure funded traders, including people who had never made a withdrawal from the forex market before.

The other reason you're going to love this is because I'm a straight shooter. I tell it like it is.

The Good, the Bad and the Ugly.

And I'm absolutely obsessed with getting frustrated forex traders the kind of results that they want.

In this guide, you're going to get very clear on all of the problems that have held you back from consistently pulling profits from the market.

How do I know?

Because I've personally spent hundreds, if not a few thousand hours personally overcoming the same problems you have, as well as helping traders just like you do the same thing.

And one thing that I can say I've gathered from all of the hours spent documenting my losses...

As well as the losses and frustrations of other traders...

Is that there were sickeningly obvious patterns and similarities between us that kept leading to the lackluster results that we all got tired of seeing.

The sad truth is: We live in a world full of people promising you the sun, the moon and the stars and failing to deliver.

But my goal in this short book is to prove to you that I not only know what the heck I'm talking about, but that I can absolutely help you get the results you want as a Forex Trader.

If you follow the steps that I'm about to give you, then you will see a radical shift in your current situation and get crystal clear on what must be done in order to consistently win in the markets.

You'll also learn that I'm the creator of my own personal method to get forex traders out of the place where they're constantly giving money to the markets...

...and into a place where they are consistently pulling profits from the markets, by leveraging large amounts of other people's capital.

This method is called **The 6-Figure Forex Trader Blueprint** and it's broken down through my Course and Coaching Accelerator: **The Magnetic Pips System.**

This system teaches traders just like you to properly Approach, Read, Dissect, Understand and Profitably Trade the Forex Market...

Consistently...

...and at Will.

- **Without using all of the old outdated methods that 99% of retail traders use and fail with...**

- **Without draining your bank account on signal services that fail to perform...**

- **And without depending on bots that always end up getting beat by the market and blowing your account.**

With that said, let's dive into the eight reasons why you haven't replaced your full time job income as a forex trader yet...

And how to fix it **fast.**

The 1st Reason

Little to No Understanding of Fundamental Drivers

REASON No. 1:
Little to No Understanding of Fundamental Drivers

Most forex traders have little to no understanding of the **Fundamental Drivers** that move the markets and many of them have been told to "Not Trade the News."

What is a **Fundamental Driver**, you ask?

A **Fundamental Driver** is an Economic Event that causes the value of a country's currency to go up or down.

To make it even easier to understand, when a **Fundamental Driver** is released as a News Event and it makes a currency's value "go down," you'll often see the market SELL that currency and BUY the other currencies attached to it.

If it makes a currency's value "go up," you'll often see the markers BUY that currency and SELL the other currencies attached to it.

Here's an Example:

Fundamental Driver: Federal Reserve Interest Rates

News Release: Interest Rates in the United States Go Up by 75 Basis Points

Currency in Question: United States Dollar (USD)

Impact on Currency Value: The United States Dollar (USD) INCREASES in value.

Impact on Currency Pair: **SELLS on EUR/USD, GBP/USD, AUD/USD, NZD/USD etc.**

Knowing this ALONE will improve your trading ten-fold.

But most Forex Traders have no idea how to interpret **Fundamental Drivers** or how to use them to their advantage. They're just taught to log on to TradingView or MetaTrader, to "Mark Up" a chart, using lines and boxes and trade what they see.

The truth is, if you try to trade the markets by just coming to a chart, drawing boxes around "zones" and trying to connect points on a trend line with "a line of most touches..."

...then you're going to consistently fail because...

Knowing what's actually moving a currency pair in a specific direction will remain a mystery to you.

You'll ultimately get fed up with doing all the things that some Forex guru told you to do before entering the market and quit without getting back all of the money you lost.

I've seen it over and over again.

You learn a "strategy" or "new approach" and get super excited, believing THIS is the thing that's going to lead to your breakthrough.

You follow the rules of this new strategy step by step and enter a position...

You see your trades go slightly into profit, then (seemingly out of nowhere) they go completely against you and drain your account.

This was something that consistently happened to one of my students, Roman, before he got really clear on what a

Fundamental Driver was and how it impacted the strength or weakness of a specific currency.

Before then, he was on the edge of giving up. He admitted that he was running the risk of causing irreparable damage to his marriage; due to the amount of money he'd lost in the market and on courses that failed to deliver consistent profits.

But once I taught him how to read and understand the **Fundamental Drivers** that made a currency strong or weak...

He was able to see an almost instantaneous shift in his results.

Instead of trying to trade the market from a one dimensional approach, he became focused on understanding the market from a multi-dimensional perspective and was able to catch some massive moves on his funded account.

In fact, once he started mastering **Fundamental Drivers**, he was able to earn in a matter of days what it used to take him an entire month to earn at his corporate six figure job.

The process that I recommend is really simple:

Learn how to interpret **Fundamental Analysis** and understand **Fundamental Drivers** immediately!

That way, you can begin to understand what is going to give power to specific currencies or take power away from specific currencies…

So that you can exploit that currency's strength or weakness against another.

For example: One **Fundamental Driver** that I teach all of my traders to pay attention to is the **Core Consumer Price Index**, because it's a measure of a country's inflation.

When my students realize that a country's level of inflation is rising, they immediately begin to evaluate that country's currency and try to pair it with another country's currency where their inflation is either stagnant or declining.

By doing this, they are able to catch massive trending moves; allowing them to earn substantial profits with minimal risks.

I have an easy step by step process that helps traders understand the **Fundamental Drivers** that are moving the market.

These are drivers that you can follow so that you can become a market participant with the big fish that move the money in the forex market.

In all honesty, this is one of my best kept secrets and is closely guarded by everyone in my community that has access to this information.

However, if you want to improve your trading faster, I would strongly suggest getting a coach that can teach you easy ways to understand **Fundamental Analysis**, and give you constant feedback on whether or not you're truly grasping the concepts.

This will help you execute like a highly paid professional, much sooner than later.

Don't waste your time scouring the internet and trying to piecemeal information together using free YouTube videos. Especially because 99% of the free content that you find online is shallow or incomplete.

It is only meant to pique your curiosity and lead you down a rabbit hole so that YouTube content creators can get more views, keep you on the YouTube platform longer and get paid by advertisers.

Always Remember This: The more time you spend on YouTube, the more money advertisers make.

The truth is, the more time you spend on YouTube or trying to piece together tidbits of free information from unreliable online sources, the more it will dilute your focus, confuse you and negatively impact your results.

The quickest way to get better is to work with one professional that truly understands what the market drivers are and is able to teach you in plain, non-esoteric, easy to understand language.

Throughout this book, you'll learn just how easy it is to get that kind of help without it costing you an arm and a leg.

It goes without saying that the easier it is to understand a concept, the more likely you are to implement what you're learning and see it work; thus improving your trading, while also decreasing your chances of getting distracted by something else.

The 2nd Reason
Little to No Clear Understanding of Smart Money Concepts

REASON No. 2:
Little to No Clear Understanding of Smart Money Concepts

The truth is, one of the biggest reasons forex traders fail to catch large moves without getting stopped out and losing their money first is because they don't truly understand Who Smart Money is, How Smart Money Moves and When to Trade with Smart Money.

If you want to be consistently successful in the markets, you must learn to focus on the few and not the many.

The vast majority of traders do the same thing. And all of those traders lose more often than they win. **They are called Dumb Money.**

A select few traders trade in a very different way. And that small percentage of traders earn all of the profits. **They are called Smart Money.**

If you see that hundreds and thousands of other traders are all being taught to do the same things, I recommend you do the exact opposite…

Because that's what Smart Money is doing.

If you don't know exactly who the Smart Money traders are and how they manipulate the market, you'll remain lost in the market and fall victim to the same Stop Loss Hunts that blow 90% to 95% of retail traders' accounts week after week.

The better you get to know who the true market movers are, their Playbook and their **4-Phase Smart Money Master Pattern**, the easier it will be to identify what the best trades to take are; especially if you don't want to be stuck in front of the charts all day.

I have a client, Candace, who had been trading for 4 years before becoming one of my students. Before she met me, she had never successfully entered and exited a profitable trade on her own. The only time she ever made any money was if and when she was lucky enough to jump in on a decent signal provided by someone else.

She was never taught **Smart Money Concepts** such as Imbalances, Liquidity Voids, Fair Value Gaps, Mitigations, Liquidity Sweeps, Session Objectives, Change of Characters or anything like that.

But what was worse was the fact that she didn't even know how to look at a chart and **recognize when Smart Money was involved** or where the best opportunities to trade were.

As she found herself losing money with all of her fellow trading friends, she realized that she'd spent years and lots of money trying to master strategies that would hardly ever work.

So I suggested that she start by learning how to **recognize the 4-Phase Smart Money Master Pattern** in the market and **only trade the 3rd and or 4th Phase** of the Pattern.

There are **hundreds** of Smart Money Concepts that you'll learn over time. But one that you can learn quickly and immediately AND use to begin improving your trading RIGHT NOW is the **4-Phase Smart Money Master Pattern.**

If you've never heard of, or seen, the **4-Phase Smart Money Master Pattern,** allow me to break it down for you here.

Phase 1: The Accumulation

This is a stage where the market is giving you what looks like a very clear Support and Resistance Level. If you were to draw a rectangular box around the price action on your chart, you'd see a very clean "Price Ceiling and Price Floor.

This is an "okay" environment to trade if you're just looking to "Sell the Ceilings and Buy the Floors," but you have to know that this phase is just a set up for the next move.

Phase 2: The Manipulation

This is a stage where the market "breaks out" below the Support Level or above the Resistance Level. Many uneducated traders try to jump in on these seemingly explosive trades for a big and fast move.

Only to find out that this move will be short lived and if they don't take their profits quickly, they're going to get hurt really badly.

This is an environment where I teach my traders to wait and "Prepare for the Long Ride."

Phase 3: The True Move

This is a stage where the market "suddenly" turns around, ending the breakout and begins to trend in the opposite direction. The trend usually consists of 3 to 5 "pushes" that cause a Break of Structure with each new push.

Phase 4: The Trend Reversal

This is a stage where the market reaches the end of the trend and turns price back around to sweep at least 50% of the Trend Line Liquidity that was created during Phase 3.

I taught this to Candace and showed her how to properly identify and trade it.

She focused on finding and recognizing the **4-Phase Smart Money Master Pattern** on all time frames and selected the time frames that worked best for her lifestyle, as well as her individual patience level.

In less than 4 weeks, she began to independently catch profitable trades on her own while actually spending less time on the charts because she was only focused on finding a few specific things in the market each week.

Within 90 days, she'd doubled her live trading account twice.

If you'd like to actually see this explained in further detail as well as a few examples of this on the charts, I've created a special bonus video training, just for people that bought this book.

Simply go to **www.SmartMoneyMasterPattern.com** and check out the free video training for yourself.

The 3rd Reason
You Have No Trade Entry Formula

REASON No. 3:
You Have No Trade Entry Formula

The truth is, most traders make terrible entries.

Almost all traders enter the market way too late or way too early and suffer a lengthy period of drawdown. However, this isn't the real issue. And this is where you should get excited!

The truth is, by having a systematic, step by step process to define exactly **when, where, how and what time** you enter your trades, your entries will begin to stand head and shoulders above your peers.

One of my clients, Phil, mentioned that almost all of his trades went right into depressing levels of drawdown as soon as he entered his trades.

And the worst part was, he would manually close his trades at a loss and walk away his charts…

Only to come back to the charts later and see that the trade would have gone his way and hit his Take Profit Level.

Has that ever happened to you?

Admittedly, it used to happen to me all the time, when I first got started trading.

Once Phil became a client, I taught him how to stack **7 specific confluences** and marry those confluences with specific entry triggers at certain times of the day.

Exactly 6 months and three days later, Phil was a 6-Figure Funded Trader, passing his $100,000 Funding Challenge with MyForex Funds on the very first try.

This resulted in him having a clearly defined exit strategy from a job that he hated and more time for his daughter.

When you don't have a clearly defined, step by step and systematic way to make an entry decision, then your trades will almost always suffer long periods of heart wrenching drawdown. And many times, you'll even get stopped out before the trade goes your way.

This is where I see most traders throw in the towel because they feel like they'll never be good enough to make money in the markets and that their hard work will never pay off.

Most traders are never taught to wait for specific "signals" or "triggers" to present themselves in the market, before entering a trade. And an even smaller number is taught to wait for multiple signals to present themselves at the same time before entering.

But if you focus on following a proven trade entry checklist, you'll find that catching larger moves for substantial profits will become second nature.

For example: One part of my signature trade entry formula is finding a very clear 3 candle price action pattern such as a Rally Base Rally or Drop Base Drop at the 79% Fibonacci Retracement Level.

When a pattern like this shows up, at this particular Fibonacci Retracement Level; no matter what pair I'm trading, I immediately prepare to enter the trade (as long as it's during an active trading session.) I also make sure I have a clear understanding of the **Fundamental Drivers** for that day and week.

Once I get my other 2 to 3 confirmations, I confidently enter the trade (expecting a risk to reward of at least 1 to 8 RR) and I share the trade idea with my private clients.

But because each of them has learned my trade entry formula for themselves during my Course and Coaching Accelerator, **The Magnetic Pips System**, many of them will have already entered the trade even before I sent the signal out.

By doing this, they are able to catch very low risk, high reward trades.

I have a simple checklist that I follow and give to each of my clients that helps us know exactly **when, where, why and how** we should enter High Probability, Low Risk and High Reward trades. These are steps that you can also follow so that you can begin making better entries quickly and suffer little to no drawdown.

To be fair, it took a lot of blown accounts and heartache to finally figure this out. And now that we have something that's proven to work time and time again, we guard it like precious jewels.

If your goal is to make better trading decisions and have crispier entries that go blue almost instantly, I think it would be wise to develop your own trade entry checklist and formula. Once you've done this, back test it at least 500 times and make sure that it has at least a 50% win rate with a minimum Risk to Reward Profile of 1 to 2.5 RR.

Either do that or **borrow one that's already been battle tested and proven to be profitable.** This will move you a step closer to becoming a consistently profitable trader, much sooner than later.

Just don't waste your money paying for signals or bots anymore.

Especially because every bot that I've ever seen created has eventually been beaten by the market and every signal caller that I know has been cooked at least once by their favorite pair.

Instead of relying on a computer program that can't interpret **Fundamental Drivers** or someone else's analysis, become your own signal by mastering a profitable trade entry formula.

The truth is, it doesn't matter how many people are in a trading community with you or who leads it.

> *"At some point, you're going to have to learn how to walk up to a chart all by yourself and take a profit earning position without someone telling you."*
> **- Coach MJ Worthmore**

And your ability to do that <u>consistently</u> is what will set you apart from all of your other trading buddies and make you the envy of the group.

QUESTION FROM THE AUTHOR: Do You Want to Work with a Multiple 6 Figure Trader until you become one yourself?

If so, go to **www.LCACoachingCall.com** to book your Coaching Call, and you'll learn exactly how to finally make it happen. Use Coupon Code: **Save99** to take 99% off of the Normal Retail Price.

The 4th Reason
You Have No Trade Management Plan

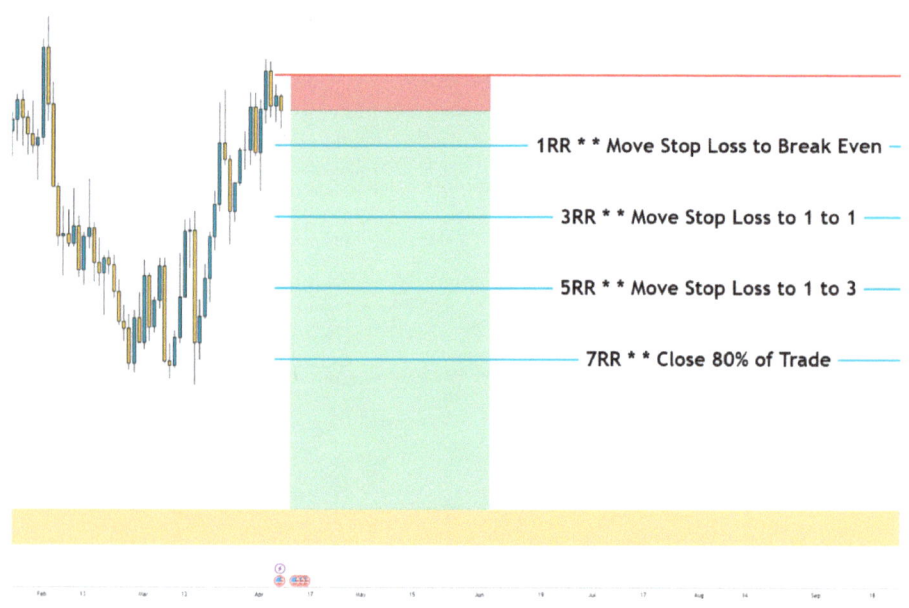

REASON No. 4:
You Have No Trade Management Plan

One of the worst things to do as a trader is enter a trade and not have a **Pre-Existing Trade Management Plan**.

But the truth is, if you ask 100 retail traders what their **Pre-Existing Trade Management Plan** is...

99 of them will look at you as if you have three heads.

Without having a **Pre-Existing Trade Management Plan** that governs exactly when, where and how you **protect your profits or close a bad trade**...

You will always run the risk of losing more money than you make and even worse...

Watching a once profitable trade turn Red.

One of my most recent clients, Andrew, told me over dinner once that he had never even heard of a **Pre-Existing Trade Management Plan** before becoming a student of **The Magnetic Pips System.**

To add insult to injury, he felt as though he was a slave to his charts, because he was always watching his trades play out instead of allowing his alerts to work for him and keep his stress levels low.

Once he became a client, I taught him how to enter his trades with confidence using my **LCA Trade Entry Formula.** But I also showed him how to set specific alerts at specific points so that he could allow the trades to play out the way they were always going to play out, whether he entered the trade or not.

Within his first 60 days of using my **Pre-Existing Trade Management Plan,** he was spending less time trading, with little to no stress at all and was loving the fact that alerts came to his cell phone letting him know how deep his trades were in profit...

Or if he needed to cut a position off and re-evaluate his decision, without it taking too much of his money.

This resulted in him passing his simulated funded trader challenge three times back to back and stepping into his live $200,000 Challenge with MyForexFunds with absolute confidence and assurance that he would pass on his first try.

Without a **Pre-Existing Trade Management Plan**, you also run the risk of letting a trade move into profit, pullback beyond your original entry point and stop you out…

Causing you to take an unnecessary loss before the trade moves in your overall direction.

Also without a clearly defined **Trade Management Plan**, you run the risk of marrying your analysis and committing the deadly sin of being patient with your losers and impatient with your winners.

This is exactly why 90% of forex traders blow their accounts.

Not just because they don't know how to trade in the correct direction of the market, but when they are lucky enough to enter into good trades, they don't have a **Pre-Existing Trade Management Plan** that allows them to scale in and out of positions profitably, while also protecting their growing profits.

And because traders are not taught to **be patient with their winners and impatient with their losers**, they suffer large amounts of drawdown; which damages their psychology. Or they take many unnecessary losses and sacrifice their equity account.

The benefit to having a proven and easy to follow **Trade Management Plan** is that you will learn to let your winners run and you'll experience the joy of seeing much larger profits instead of closing a winning trade too soon...

Only to look up and see that if you had held on for just a bit longer, you would have made 2, 3 or even 5 times as much as you settled for.

By focusing on making this shift, you'll not only achieve the financial rewards of the elite traders that you admire, but also the peace and tranquility that they experience on a regular basis.

A part of my **Trade Management Plan** is I get an alert once my trade is in profit, three times the size of my risk.

For example, if I take a trade that has a $100 total risk, I get alerted when that trade is $300 in profit.

If this particular trade is a trade that I believe has a $1,000 potential (which is a 1 to 10 Risk/Reward profile trade), then I will move my stop loss to either break even, so that I can't lose any money...

Or I'll move my stop loss to 1 to 1 and to secure the amount of money that I risked. So even if the trade pulls back, I still come out on top, earning the same $100 that I originally risked. So not only did I not lose any money, but I've also earned $100 that I can use later for a different trade opportunity.

This allows me and my students to move our stop losses based on structure and remove the emotional attachment from the money.

I also like to be alerted when my trade has reached a specific level of drawdown.

Because when you know that your trade has moved too much in the opposite direction of your entry, you can evaluate the position and choose to close it early for a small loss instead of a bigger one, and also look to see if you're upside down on your analysis.

Many times this has saved my students from staying in bad trades, allowing them to cut a loss early and trade in the proper direction of the market; gaining back their small loss and also catching a big win.

In my Course and Coaching Accelerator, **The Magnetic Pips System**, I teach all of my students how to design their own **Trade Management Plans** based on their individual risk profile, lifestyle and personal level of patience. I also teach them that not all trades are handled the same.

A trade that has a 1 to 4 risk/reward ratio profile is not managed the same as a trade with a 1 to 10 risk/reward ratio profile. So by knowing the difference between their trades, they also know when, where and why to secure their profits.

Not every trader wants to take what we do in the forex market seriously and somehow, many still believe that this is a get rich quick scheme, where they can put $50 into an account and compounded it into $5 million in just a matter of a few short weeks.

But if you're one of the traders that now understands that this is a fallacy and that trading requires patience, discipline and mastery, then it only makes sense that you either develop or borrow a **Trade Management Plan** that will allow you to:

⁰ Kill your losers quickly

⁰ Let your winners run and ultimately...

⁰ Live by your alerts

There's literally no point to executing a trade and then staring at the charts for hours on end, causing your blood pressure to go up and running the risk of having a heart attack. Especially when the highest paid traders in the world don't do that. The best traders place their positions, place their stops, take profits and also place their alerts.

And once they're done, they walk away from their monitors and oftentimes go get martinis.

Some of the best experiences I've ever had was placing a trade and walking away from the charts just to get an alert a few hours later, saying *"Your trade has reached a profit level of 5 times the risk. Close 90% of the position, move stop loss into profit at 2RR and let the rest play out…"*

All while sitting at a bar with my friends, eating an order of wings and sipping on my favorite whisky.

And this is the reality that I want for you…

Unless, of course, you prefer martinis.

The 5th Reason
You Have No Clear Understanding of Risk to Reward Ratios

REASON No. 5:
You Have No Clear Understanding of Risk to Reward Ratios

Have you ever gotten a signal that said something like this?

Sell GBP/USD
 ° Stop Loss: **50 pips**

 ° TP1: 15 pips
 ° TP2: 30 pips
 ° TP3: 45 pips
 ° TP4: **60 pips**

...and etc?

This is the equivalent to someone saying:

"***Risk $50**, but feel free to close your trade when it is **$15**, **$30** or **$45** in profit. And the big goal (if you don't close the trade at any of those points) is **$60.***"

Every trader I know has seen and even taken a signal like this. And I can tell you without a shadow of a doubt that signals like these have caused more traders to blow their accounts than the law should allow.

But why?

The answer is because if you look at a signal like that, you'll notice that the stop losses were always significantly larger than the first 1 to 3 take profit points, where a trader was told to either completely take profit or take a partial profit on their trade.

The difficult part about this is the fact that most traders are trading small amounts of capital. Because of this, they can't even safely trade with lot sizes large enough to take partials.

This proves that new traders come into the game being taught to risk substantially more than what they are potentially taking as a reward.

And the problem with this is: when the risk to reward profile is **lopsided against you**, it will always lead to a disastrous outcome.

For example, a new trader is told whenever a signal is sent out, to **risk $50** on that particular trade and take profit when their trade **has only earned $15.**

The trader takes 10 signals and "wins" 7 of them, earning $15 each time, for a total of $105.

The other 3 trades go against them, however. And with each loss, they lose $50, totaling $150 is losses.

This wipes out 100% of that trader's earnings and even puts them in the **negative $45;** even though the trader had a 70% "win rate."

On the flip side, a professional trader trades the opposite way.

In the same scenario, they will take 10 trades, risking only $15, but accepting nothing less than a reward of $50.

Let's say that the professional trader loses 7 trades out of 10 trades at $15 per loss and wins 3 out of 10 trades at $50 per win.

This means the pro would have lost $105 from the 7 losses.

But because they won 3 trades, earning $50 each time, the $105 in losses are completely covered by the $150 in earnings, giving that trader a **$45 profit**; even though they only have a 30% win rate.

Here's the question that I would ask you.

If you had to choose: Would you rather have a high win rate and lose money, or a low win rate and consistently earn a profit?

I hope that you would choose to have a low win rate and earn a profit rather than the alternative. Because as the saying goes, *"You don't always have to get it right in order to get rich."*

Many traders profess to have high win rates, when in reality, they're just traders that trade with upside down risk to reward ratio profiles, where the risk they take on is much larger than the rewards they should accept.

I've helped each of my clients to understand this, so that they know as long as their risk/reward ratio profiles are lopsided in their favor, they will almost always come out with profit at the end.

Naturally, a trader can improve their Win Rate by knowing more things about the market, such as **Fundamental Analysis, Smart Money Concepts and Entry Triggers.** But at the end of the day, trading is a game of probabilities.

You will have losses and you will have wins.

But this is the only game of probabilities where you get to **predetermine** the size of your losses and the size of your wins.

Traders that won't last long in the game will always risk more than they can afford to lose. But the traders that will stand the test of time and earn obscene amounts of money, only trade with lopsided risk/reward ratio profiles that work in their favor.

One of my clients, Marsha, used to struggle with this.

She was taught to give her trades large amounts of "breathing room" so that the trade could go against her and then (at some point) go in her direction. While there is some truth to this, the way she was taught was that **her trades needed to have more breathing room than necessary.**

To add salt to the wound, she was also taught to close the trade once she saw just a little bit of profit.

Once she became a client of mine, she began to see profits that she'd never seen before within her first six weeks, simply because I helped her understand the value of making sure her potential rewards were always larger than the risks she took on.

As an aspiring professional, this allows you to successfully earn income from the markets while also losing with grace. We know that losses are inevitable, but it's our job to make sure that all losses are controllable and manageable.

For example, I have all of my students go through a powerful exercise that even you can do, right now, to prove that this concept will work in your favor…

But ONLY if you follow my exact instructions.

For this exercise you'll need a piece of paper, a pen and a coin to flip.

On that piece of paper, draw a line down the center.

On the left hand side, write the word "Heads" and on the right hand side write the word "Tails."

Then I want you to flip the coin 100 times.

Whenever the coin lands on Heads, I want you to write down **+$30** under the Heads column.

Whenever the coin lands on tails, I want you to write down **- $10** under the Tails column.

I have had every single one of my 200+ students do this exercise, and the results were unanimous. On average, traders would have a 50% win rate. But even when traders had a lower win rate, they still came out profitable.

And it was the traders that had more losses than winners that received the biggest lesson.

These traders, with the lower win rates, would lose (on average) 65 of the coin flips and win 35 of the coin flips.

This means, the average trader would lose about $650 due to the 65 losses at $10 each.

But the other 35 wins gave the traders $30 each, totaling $1,050 in wins.

They would see that even though they had only a 35% win rate, they had still earned a profit of $400

All of a sudden, each trader realized that it made more sense to **only** take trades where the reward was at least three times the size of the risk they were willing to take on. This allowed them to have a "less than stellar" Win Rate and still make money.

With work, a proven system and coaching, your Win Rate will naturally improve. But even before then, a trader can learn to realize and appreciate the power (and the profit) is in the Risk/Reward Ratio Profile.

Understanding this alone will allow you to ultimately come out on top.

When you don't truly understand lopsided risk/reward ratio trading, you fall victim to incorrect thinking and poor trade selection.

But I can guarantee you when you shift your focus to learning a style of trading where the rewards are always significantly larger than the risk that you're willing to take on, you'll see a significant boost in your profits and account equity in very short order.

For example in my Course and Coaching accelerator, **The Magnetic Pips System**, I teach all of my students how to identify a 1 to 5 Risk to Reward Ratio trade at least once a week; meaning for every $1 they risk, there is **minimum** of $5 in potential rewards on the other side.

By doing so, I can just about guarantee that my traders will be profitable every month.

Even with an "average" win rate of 40% - 50%, traders are able to walk away with "Real Money" and consistently request payouts.

Simply because they are constantly focused on trading with proper and professional, Risk/Reward Ratio Profiles...

Where the reward is ALWAYS lopsided in their favor.

QUESTION FROM THE AUTHOR: Do You Want to Work with a Multiple 6 Figure Trader until you become one yourself?

If so, go to **www.LCACoachingCall.com** to book your Coaching Call, and you'll learn exactly how to finally make it happen. Use Coupon Code: **Save99** to take 99% off of the Normal Retail Price.

The 6th Reason

Little to No Understanding of How to Control Risk

REASON No. 6:
Little to No Understanding of How to Control Risk

This chapter alone can make you wealthy as a trader, if you pay close attention to what you're about to read and actually implement it.

I know this because after working with hundreds of unprofitable traders, I noticed that close to 100% would all say, at some point…

"I was on a hot streak and earning a lot of money. And then… in just a few trades, **I lost it all plus more.***"*

Almost every trader goes through this.

And the truth is… going through this devastating experience is completely unnecessary and easily avoidable.

Almost all traders that have blown an account have seen their profits diminish faster than they earned them. What they don't know is that this issue can be fixed simply and quickly, if they learned how to count pips and weigh their pip's value.

This is the 1st key to learning **How to Control Risk.**

Most traders simply don't know how to count pips or weigh the pip value for the pair they're trading. But even that isn't the real issue. And therein lies your opportunity to rise above the unsuccessful masses.

The truth is, by learning how to count pips and weigh the pip value for the pair you're trading, you can professionally calculate the size of any position you take. And by having a simplified way to calculate the value of your position, (based on a reasonable stop loss and a predetermined risk amount) you'll easily beat the 95% of traders that blow their accounts and never even turn a profit.

But what truly gives the elite traders their edge is the fact that **they are emotionally unattached from the outcome of any one trade.**

No single trade defines us, therefore no single trade can defeat us.

One of my clients, Chris, used to fall victim to this over and over again.

Things had gotten so bad for him that he openly cried on a 1-on-1 Zoom call with me. To make matters worse, he was slightly upside down on some of his major monthly expenses and was afraid that he would soon drown in personal debt.

Once he became a client, I helped to re-prioritize some things with his personal finances and make some tough but necessary decisions. Because of our chat, he was able to recoup a good portion of the money he lost, regain peace of mind and take the pressure off of his trading.

Within his first 90 days, he'd grown a small account with just $115 in it to over $1,000, using proper risk management and never over leveraging on a single position.

This resulted in his confidence hitting an all time high and it also allowed him to have an all expenses paid Daddy-daughter mini-vacation using his Forex Profits.

He's now training for his funded challenge, using the exact same risk control and risk management techniques that I taught him. And I absolutely expect him to knock out his first 6-Figure Funded Challenge with speed and ease.

Without learning how to let go of your emotional attachment to the money that you could lose or earn on any given trade, you'll always end up over-leveraging on positions and running the risk of losing all of your hard earned profits in a very short period of time.

This is where almost every trader asks the defining questions that makes or breaks their career:

"Is this really for me?"

"Can I really do this?"

"Will I ever make any money doing this?"

"Should I just... quit?"

Of all of the courses I've purchased and gone through over the years, I've never heard an "educator" or "guru" clearly articulate exactly HOW to manage risk with each individual position a trader takes...

Or exactly HOW a trader can train themselves on letting go of their "need" to win a trade and make money.

But if you can focus on learning and mastering these skills, you'll never worry about making money as a forex trader, ever again.

For example: Each of my traders knows that before they execute a single trade, on any given trading day, they must already have a predetermined amount that they're ok with losing for that day. This amount must also be

negligible in relation to their account balance, so they're able to trade without fear of major losses.

For my 300k funded traders, they typically will not risk more than $1,500 in a single trading day, and will not accept a reward less than $4,500 once their position is placed.

They also know that putting the entire $1,500 predetermined risk for the day on a single position or a single currency pair isn't very wise, so they'll typically risk about $500 on a position and take no more than 3 positions, that day, across different pairs.

This allows them to see their positions as a fraction of 1%... a number that is easily re-attainable, should any of the trades they place turn against them.

Finally, they know exactly how to do the math and find out the appropriate lot size for the position they want to take, regardless of the currency pair they are trading.

By trading this way, they get to keep their peace and still earn significant income with losses included.

You can very easily do the same thing.

I teach all of my traders the exact step by step process that I use to manage my risk and keep it under control.

Most importantly, I also teach them how to manage their personal finances and money mindset, so that they're never stressed about how much money they will make or lose on a trade.

I do this by teaching them how to skillfully and enjoyably live beneath their means, while also teaching them additional ways to earn income aside from trading. This allows earning profits as a trader to become a lot easier.

In truth, I got the idea from Warren Buffet.

Everyone knows Warren Buffet as the greatest investor of all time... but very few people seem to know that before he became the world's greatest investor, he taught investing tactics at a local college.

He used the money he earned from his "job" to keep his bills paid and invest in the markets.

As we know, that plan worked out pretty well for him, long term. And even now, as a multi-billionaire, he lives waaaay beneath his means.

If you have a goal of becoming a trader that can always look forward to a handsome payout from the Prop Firm of your choosing; whether that's every two weeks or every 30 days, learning **How to Control Risk** is a non-negotiable.

Without it, hoping to ever get paid like the best in the business is a childish dream.

Start learning **How to Control Risk** by giving yourself a predetermined risk amount for each day and each trade. Also, remember that not all standard lots are created equal, especially when changing from major pairs to crosses, metals or indices. And above all else, do everything in your power to remove your emotional connection from the need to win the trade.

The truth is, it doesn't matter how many times you take a losing trade. At some point, you're going to have a string of winners and finally find your edge. And once you do, all of your winners will pay for your losers and you'll never lose another wink of sleep because of a small dent in your account balance.

A saying that we live by at LCA University is,

"Before you learn to win with ease, you have to learn to lose with grace."
- Coach MJ Worthmore

And trading with well controlled risk will allow you to do just that.

QUESTION FROM THE AUTHOR: Do You Want to Work with a Multiple 6 Figure Trader until you become one yourself?

If so, go to **www.LCACoachingCall.com** to book your Coaching Call, and you'll learn exactly how to finally make it happen. Use Coupon Code: **Save99** to take 99% off of the Normal Retail Price.

The 7th Reason

You Have No *"Walk Away from the Table"* Number

REASON No. 7:
You Have No "Walk Away from the Table" Number.

This chapter goes hand in hand with the previous chapter.

While knowing **How to Control Risk** is extremely important, what's even more important is knowing when to **Walk Away** from your trading desk after having cleared your screen.

As we've already discussed: Losses Are Inevitable in Trading. But the truth is, by having a **Walk Away from the Table Number**, you can allow yourself to take the time you need to recover from any tolls that losses take on your mind and emotions.

One of my clients, MeSean, used to have an issue with "Revenge Trading."

As an extremely competitive person, who loves to win and he constantly pushes himself to continually be better at everything that he does. So naturally, losing trades and spiraling out of control because of it was something that he was constantly struggling with.

To add insult to injury, he would not only take losses and immediately try to make his money right back…

But he would also take bigger and bigger positions with each new trade, in hopes of catching just a small move to help him recover whatever was lost.

When he became a client, I taught him how to address the emotional side of losing trades and how to strategically see each loss as a lesson in the market. I also taught him that once he hit a certain amount of money lost in a single day, that he had to clear off his charts and walk away.

But instead of just walking away and "stewing" in defeat, he needed to go and immediately do something else that he was good at or something that he enjoyed doing, to help bring him back to a level head.

This resulted in him not only saving his account, but also spending more time doing the deep work of reinforcing positive feelings about himself; especially locking in on a mindset that I teach all of my clients.

> *"Just because you have a bad trading day, doesn't mean that you're a bad trader."*
> - **Coach MJ Worthmore**

By coming to clean charts, with fresh eyes, the next day, he would be able to see if and when he was upside down on his analysis or if his entry was just a little too early. He would then place trades in the right direction (with proper risk management, of course) and make back the money he lost, plus profits.

When you don't have a set **Walk Away from the Table Number**, as most Blackjack players call it, you run the risk of increasing the size of the hole in your trading account.

This is where I see many traders go on what seems to be a **never ending losing streak**, where their emotions get the best of them and in a single day, they sacrifice their entire account.

Most traders are never taught to come to each trading day with a set number that they are okay with losing, nor do they have a plan of action that tells them exactly when to walk away from their charts and what to do once they've walked away.

But if you focus on remembering that trading is a game of probabilities where you will lose some and you will win some, as long as the outcome is that you've earned income...

You'll be fine.

Especially if you have a small predetermined amount (relative to your account size) that you will not exceed in losses on any given trading day.

For me, whenever I have a losing day, I go play basketball.

Why?

Because I'm a very good basketball player. And by going to a court and shooting hoops, watching the ball go through the net, it reminds me that I'm good at things that I work at.

After I play basketball, I spend time with my son and daughter watching Disney movies.

Why?

Because by spending time with my children and seeing them enjoy time with their Daddy, I'm reminded that a loss for the day is only temporary. And there are more important things in life than money.

Even though the money is good and necessary to pay for our lifestyle, I'm reminded that I can be happy every day, even though I didn't get the trading result that I was looking for that day.

Quite frankly, this was one of the hardest lessons for me to learn because I never had a coach to tell me how to determine what my **Walk Away Number** was or what to do when I had a bad trading day.

Nonetheless, this was a lesson that I learned out of necessity and desperation.

So if you have ambitions on being a trader that knows **regardless** of the inevitable losses that you'll take, that you will still end your trading period with a substantial paycheck…

Then you must have a **Walk Away from the Table Number**.

The truth is, even the best traders in the world, have bad trading days and go on losing streaks. But because they have clearly defined **Walk Away from the Table Numbers**, they know (beyond the shadow of a doubt) that profits are just around the corner.

All they need is a few good setups to make everything right again.

Your willingness to accept and implement this will quickly make you a titan in the Forex Trading Industry.

The 8th Reason

You Have No Coach to Take You to the Next Level

REASON No. 8:
You Have No Coach to Take You to the Next Level

This final chapter is all about the single thing that can make or break a trader, as well as any other highly paid professional, in any arena.

Every trader that's still pressing toward the goal of big wins and large profits, seems to forget one thing...

That every seemingly "exceptionally skilled" master of this craft was once a Know-Nothing Student to a master themselves.

The truth is...

Trading with the hopes of earning a substantial income, without having a dedicated coach is the highest level of idiocy and naivete.

But you don't want just "any ole" Coach. You need a coach that can skillfully mentor you and teach you what you need to know about the markets. And that same coach also needs to help you identify the chinks in your armor so you can strengthen your weaknesses over time.

But the sad truth is: Not all coaches are created equal.

Have you ever seen a trader hire "coaches" or "mentors," and pay good money, just to hear that "coach" ran off and never owned up to the promises that they made?

They never truly educate the student that they took the money from, nor do they stay by the student's side until that student gets the specific result that they were looking for.

Over the last few years, I've seen this happen time and time again. And it's one of the main reasons why I personally offer **Results Based Guarantees in writing and via video recording** to each of my Course and Coaching Accelerator clients.

Because, as a trading coach, I believe that it's my responsibility to make sure my traders see a **return of** their investment and a significant return on their investment. Most importantly, I believe their success (or lack thereof) is a direct reflection of me.

Personally, I refuse to let my reputation be a bad one.

My father taught me early in my life that *"A good name is better than silver and gold… and a man's reputation is more valuable than the money in his pocket."*

In fact, every single one of my clients has heard me say,

"If you decide to work with me, the only way that you won't become successful is if you quit! Because I will only ever share with you the things that I have proven works time and time again. Furthermore, I promise to teach you in ways that help you understand and duplicate the successful things that I do."

When you look at all of the greats in sports and academia, each of the giants that we have grown to know and love, all stand on the shoulders of their mentors and coaches.

Both Michael Jordan and Kobe Bryant; arguably two of the best basketball players to ever play the game, were both trainees and mentees of Tim Grover.

The greatest known neurosurgeon in the world, Dr. Bartolome Oliver accredits his skill, knowledge and accolades to his mentor, Dr. Sixto Obrador.

And even the world's greatest investor of all time, Warren Buffett, openly admits that he would not be who he is without his mentor, Benjamin Graham.

Every successful person has a successful coach and mentor.

Even my mentor has a mentor.

And I know that I've become who I am, as both a trader and a trainer because I've been directly coached by industry leaders; leaders whose results have far exceeded mine (for now).

But over the years, what I've learn by having a good coach is:

When you get the right one, you not only get their personal knowledge, wisdom and experience, but you also get the knowledge, wisdom and experience of the coaches and mentors that developed them...

Without having to pay the prices they paid!

Furthermore, it's my opinion that the absolute best coaches are the ones that take personal responsibility for your success and attach their payoff to yours.

Meaning if you don't win, they don't win.

This is something that I've intentionally embedded into the payment structure of my own coaching program. And if that's not something you've ever experienced before, I would invite you to take a look at it for yourself.

But even if you chose not to work with or learn directly from me, it's still my unfailing and unchanging opinion that every trader that seeks to become the best version of themselves MUST HAVE a great coach.

One that can hold your hand and lead from the front…

And whenever necessary, stand behind you and push you toward your potential.

And once you've got to the point where you can call yourself a champion…

You'll have no problem allowing them to stand next to you and help you hold up your trophies.

Quick Question for Serious Traders?

"Would You Like to Work Together?"

DO NOT MISS OUT ON THIS

Congratulations on getting to the end of this short book!

I now want to invite you to COPY my methods and inject it into your own trading system.

Plus, I want to also give you a chance to book a 1-on-1 Coaching session with either myself or one of my teammates to help you do exactly that.

During your call with us, we'll show you exactly how to improve your trading and the exact roadmap you need to follow, in order to permanently fix the problems that are stopping you from hitting your income goals on a weekly, biweekly and monthly basis.

The truth is, if you knew what was stopping you from having $5,000, $10,000 and even $20,000+ profit months in your trading, then you would have already hit those targets. But because you haven't, that means you are most likely following the wrong method and system.

So let's change that right now!

Just a heads up, the Consultation Call is a true value of $2,500 USD. That's what we charge at a consultancy and training level.

However, we are giving you the chance to book a call for pennies on the dollar because you purchased a copy of this book.

I honestly don't know how long we will be doing this for and there's even a chance that there won't be any space on the calendar when you go to book a call.

So if you do see that we still have some spots available in the coming days or weeks, **take advantage and book today** because you may not get the opportunity again.

Book today (before we close the calendar down) so that you can get your **6-Figure Forex Trader Blueprint.** We'll make sure it's individually tailored to you and your lifestyle, so you can **Match** and **Then Replace** your full time job income with your trading profits.

It's time to turn you into the trader that you're meant to be and that your family needs you to be.

All the Best,

Coach MJ Worthmore

Go to **www.LCACoachingCall.com** to book your Call with an elite member of LCA University (or even me, Coach MJ) before all of the slots are taken.

Remember, the Normal Retail Price for a Coaching or Consultation Call is **$2,500 USD**.

But because you got a copy of this book and read it to the end, you can book a Call for 99% off.

Simply go to **www.LCACoachingCall.com** to book your Coaching Call, and you'll learn exactly how to finally bring your trading goals to fruition. Just use **Coupon Code: Save99** to take 99% off of the Normal Retail Price.

www.ingramcontent.com/pod-product-compliance
Lightning Source LLC
Chambersburg PA
CBHW040224220526
45473CB00001B/114